HEART OF THE FATHER

-Rachel Wenke-

Heart of the Father

Copyright © 2015 by Rachel Wenke

No part of this publication may be reproduced or transmitted in any form or by any means, electronic or mechanical, including photocopy, recording, or any information storage or retrieval system, without permission in writing from the author.

All scripture quotations, unless otherwise indicated, are taken from the New King James Version®. Copyright © 1982, Thomas Nelson, Inc. Used by permission. All rights reserved.

Scripture quotations marked (NIV) are taken from the Holy Bible, New International Version®, NIV®. Copyright © 1973, 1978, 1984, 2011 by Biblica, Inc.™ Used by permission of Zondervan. All rights reserved worldwide. www.zondervan.com The "NIV" and "New International Version" are trademarks registered in the United States Patent and Trademark Office by Biblica, Inc.™

National Library of Australia Cataloguing-in-Publication entry

Creator: Wenke, Rachel, author.
Title: Heart of the Father / Rachel Wenke.
ISBN: 9780994273413 (paperback)
Subjects: God--Fatherhood. Fatherhood (Christian theology), Children of God.
Dewey Number: 231.1

Printed and bound in Australia in association with
Pentecost Life Centre
PO Box 625
Helensvale, QLD AUSTRALIA 4212.

www.facebook.com/heartofthefatherbook

Thank you to my sister Sarah for proofreading this book. You are such a blessing to my life- your perseverance and faith in God are inspiring.

I also wish to thank my pastor Butrone Leyshon, for your godly encouragement in producing this book. Your ministry has had such a profound impact on my relationship with the Lord, and the development of my own personal ministry unto Him.

Thank you also to Daniel Jurekie for your valuable technical assistance in the book's cover design.

But most of all, I give all the glory to my Heavenly Father, Saviour Jesus and precious Holy Spirit - Your love is truly better than life itself. Without You I am nothing, but with You by my side, I can do all things!

Contents

Introduction 7

I Want You to Know Me 9

My Greatness 13

Boiling Over 15

Your Highest Calling 19

What Do You Treasure? 23

Captivated By You 25

Wait for Me, Treasure Me 27

Stillness 31

Living Water 35

You are My Delight 39

How I See Sin 43

The Kingdom of My Heart 47

My Kingdom in You 49

My Treasure in You 51

My Way is the Greatest 53

Layers of My Love 55

Turn to Me 59

My Love is Stronger 63

My Word 65

Looking Right Through You 67

To Know Me is to Become Like Me 69

My Beauty 71

Grounded In My Love 75

Your Invitation to the Father's Heart 79

Introduction

I will never forget the night that God the Father revealed a deep longing of His heart to me. I remember arriving home and having a sense within me to go upstairs to spend some time with the Lord. I did not know what or why, but I just knew there was something important God wanted me to receive. I went upstairs, ready and waiting in expectation. "What is it Lord?", I remember seeking in my heart.

The next thing I knew, I began to sense a heavy burden in my spirit that became heavier and heavier the more I dwelt on it. As the burden intensified, an overwhelming yearning swept over me that was so sombre yet so pure at the same time. This deep longing was welling up inside of me to the point where it felt more like an ache in my heart than anything else. My heart felt like it was beginning to break. I began to realise that this emotion was not my own - it was the yearning of the Almighty Father's heart. I had never sensed such vulnerability in Him. It was then that the Father revealed what He was truly longing for - He said softly to my heart, "**I want My children to know Me**". When He spoke, there was such emphasis on the word 'Me'. This is truly the cry of His heart- for you to know Him and to love Him.

With this burden of the Father's heart impressed upon my own, the following book was written by revelation of the Holy Spirit. Each chapter is written in first person as if the Father is speaking directly to you, being transcribed to the best that I knew how, as I sensed the Father's words being revealed to my heart by His Spirit. While this book is short, I encourage you to take your time reading it, as I believe the essence of what is on each page is coming directly from the heart of the Father unto yours.

Obviously not one book could capture the heart of the Father. Not a million times a million books could capture His heart for you, for God is indescribable and His love is infinite. The purpose of the book is to simply create a holy hunger and desire in you to seek out God *for yourself.* As you do, may you come to know the reality of Him and His love for you personally, through His Son Jesus, by the power of the Holy Spirit. Only by knowing God and His love for you, can you come to love Him in return, and fulfil the greatest commandment Jesus gave us - to love the Lord your God with all your heart, soul, strength and mind (Luke 10:27).

May the Father's heart begin to captivate yours as you read His words unto you...

I Want You to Know Me

John 17:3

"*And this is eternal life, that they may know You, the only true God, and Jesus Christ whom You have sent.*"

My precious child; I created you for a purpose. I created you with one reason in mind and one reason only- it is to know Me. I want you to know who I AM. I want you to know My heart and My love for you. If you only knew how much I long for you to know Me more. How much I long for you to know Me more, so I can touch you with more of My love; so you may receive the fullness that I have for you; so that My name and My Son's name may be glorified in you.

You have no idea and will never know just how much I yearn for you; how rich My desire is for you. Even now as you read this, I AM longing for your fellowship, your attention, your affection, your love. Your heart is the most precious treasure to Me.

Many people, even in the church, have a misconception about Me. They think that because I am the Almighty God; because of My power and omnipotence, that I do not sense pain; that I cannot feel emotion; that I am immune to it. They go about sinning, living for themselves. They do not see the effect it has on Me. They never stop to think. Believe Me, My child, you could not count the number of times My heart breaks every day. My heart is grieved and aches for My children who do not know Me; who turn away from Me and My Son Jesus because of sin.

My heart aches even more when a child of Mine believes that they know Me, but their heart is deceived, for it is far from Me. They think that they know who I AM and that all is well, but they are misguided. They do not know My heart. They know about Me, but have not experienced Me. They think they know My love, but they have not experienced My love. They have not experienced My Presence, My embrace. They sing that I am their Rock, but they do not know Me as their Rock. They are their own rock. They sing that I am their Shield, but they do not know Me as their Shield - they are shielding themselves from Me. They sing that I am their deliverer, their Strong Tower, but they continually try to deliver themselves from their pain and torment. I watch them struggle in sin and fear and doubt, declaring to the world that they know Me, but they do not know My heart.

They are satisfied by hearing what someone else has told them about Me, but I AM not satisfied by this. They go to others before they come to Me. All I want is for My children to come to Me, to come to their Father's arms so I can embrace them and share Myself with them!

I AM not satisfied until My child is in My arms and looking into My eyes, knowing Me. I AM not satisfied until *you* are looking into My eyes, looking into My heart and knowing Me. I AM not satisfied with yesterday's meeting, I want to meet with you today.

Do you know that I AM looking into your eyes right now? Do you know what I AM thinking? I love you. You are Mine. My thoughts for you never cease. My Word says they outnumber the grains of sand on the seashore; but every one of those thoughts I have towards you is saying to you, My child, My delight, "I love you". I always have and I always will. Do you want to know Me?

See also:

Psalm 139:17-18, Song of Solomon 7:10, Isaiah 43:1, 4
1 John 2:3-5; 3:1-2

My Greatness

Psalm 145:3

"Great is the LORD, and greatly to be praised; And His greatness is unsearchable."

As you seek to know My heart and come deeper inside, you will begin to grow in the revelation of My Greatness. I AM greater, stronger and more perfect than your mind can ever begin to fathom.

The revelation of My Greatness rising in you will see My power rising up in and through you. When you see My greatness, you see the insignificance of all else compared to Me; you see the futility of all that rises up against Me. Who can compare to My Greatness? What problem can come against My Greatness? No one! Nothing!

I do not know any limits. No restrictions or borders are within Me. No weakness is in Me, only strength. No restrictions, only freedom and deliverance and wide expanses of ever increasing life and glory. My Greatness is never ending. But, in My Greatness, I want to meet with you. I want to share My Greatness with you.

People who fear and doubt and disbelieve Me, who lack faith, need a greater revelation of My Greatness, and that in that Greatness of who I AM, I AM for them. With all the Greatness that is in Me, know that I hold you; I carry you; I protect you and I shield you, for you are the apple of My eye; My prized possession. With everything that I AM, I hold you. With everything that I AM, I love you. With all My Greatness, I cherish you and I will nurture and protect you.

The Greatness of My embrace is freely yours now. Simply believe and trust in the work of the cross, the power of My Son's blood, which brought you into My Greatness so you may dwell not near Me but in Me - in the midst of My Great love for you. Is there anything greater than My love for you?

See also:

Psalm 17:8, Psalm 40:5, Isaiah 40:18; 21-22; Isaiah 46:4-5, Romans 8:38-39, Philippians 2:5-11

Boiling Over

2 Timothy 3:1-5

"But know this, that in the last days perilous times will come: For men will be lovers of themselves, lovers of money, boasters, proud, blasphemers, disobedient to parents, unthankful, unholy, unloving, unforgiving, slanderers, without self-control, brutal, despisers of good, traitors, headstrong, haughty, lovers of pleasure rather than lovers of God, having a form of godliness but denying its power. And from such people turn away!"

Do you know that there is emotion in Me that is boiling over? It has been simmering for generations, but today it has reached boiling point.

To know Me, you have to understand the intensity of My passion and love for you. Mine is a love that you do not know in this world. You must remember that I AM a Jealous God. I AM a Jealous God. My intense love for you fuels a boiling hot fire within Me. A fire that burns brighter and hotter than any flame known to man. I want you all to Myself.

I want My church all to Myself. But what has she done? She has prostituted herself. She has made love to other idols and united herself with them. She comes running back to Me and I forgive her when she returns to Me and repents, but there are some who are enjoying their philandering. They enjoy the pleasure that it brings to their fallen fleshly appetites and they crave for more. They reject My Spirit; they harden their heart towards Me. These ones claim to be My children but inwardly love and lust for everything that is against Me. No! I will not tolerate it. The church has become a modern day brothel for prostitutes who are lovers of themselves and far from Me. I AM bringing this to light. I will expose their motives. Their building will come to nothing.

I AM raising up the true Church of My children, My precious Bride who will delight in only Me; who will be loyal to only Me, whose first and only true love is Me. These will be united with My Son Jesus by My Spirit and together we will commune, for this is the purpose of your creation - to be made one with Me.

This army of My lovers will do great feats for Me, but they will be greatly opposed, for they will stand against everything in this world that is against Me, and that is much! They will shine like stars amongst the darkness and My Presence will not be hidden from them. My glory will shine upon them. Many will run to their rising and be taken in by My glory which will surround them. They will come to know the true Me by My Spirit, in spirit and in truth. In holiness and fear, they will rise as one, a glorious Church without spot or wrinkle. Are you a true lover of Mine?

See also:

Deuteronomy 4:24, Isaiah 60:2-3, Jeremiah 3:6-9,20;
Daniel 12:3, 2 Corinthians 11:2-4 (NIV),
Ephesians 5:27, Revelation 19:7-9

Your Highest Calling

Matthew 22:37-38

"*Jesus said to him, 'You shall love the LORD your God with all your heart, with all your soul, and with all your mind.' This is the first and great commandment.*"

My children think that the most important thing they can do for Me is serve Me. They think they are pleasing Me the most when they are doing - busy, preaching, witnessing, praying, studying. They fail to see that what I prize as most important, what I delight in the most, is simply your love for Me.

Loving Me is your highest calling. It is all I ask of you to do for Me. All else will simply come from loving Me. When you love Me, you obey Me and My will is naturally fulfilled. Your calling and serving will naturally follow, but it comes from loving Me first. If you try to serve Me but it does not come from your love for Me, then who are you serving? Me or yourself?

You do not impress Me when you are trying to serve Me. I AM not impressed with sacrifices. I only desire you- your heart, your love; that is what I want. I long for your love. I do not long for your works or your attempts to please Me - I want you.

Your love for Me is giving yourself to Me. A life surrendered to Me in love is what I delight in. A life laid down for Me, not out of obligation or fear, but out of love. This is the life that will bear much fruit.

Love is the deepest and only root needed to be connected to Me. Without love, you are not connected to Me- your fruit has no root; it is just a shell void of any true nutrient. I reject it. The fruit I delight in is anything that is rooted in love for Me. Being rooted and grounded in love for Me, which comes from knowing Me by My Spirit, is the most important thing you can do in My eyes.

You preachers, you teachers, you ministers, hear Me now - your love for Me is more important than the sermons you preach, the books you write, and the prayers you offer. Your love for Me is the most important thing you can give Me. Remember that your first ministry is always your love for Me. Do not let your love and intimacy for Me ever move to the background as you serve Me, for you cannot serve Me except with love. Without love for Me, any service in My name you are doing for yourself, not Me.

People are preoccupied with works and service in My Name because such things can be seen to the outward world. It is proof that you are working for Me. Others cannot always see your intimacy with Me for it happens in the secret place of My heart, but I see it. Others close to

My heart will also know when you are close to My heart, for when you speak of Me they will recognise Who you speak of as the One they cherish.

There is nothing that you can do for Me that means more to Me than your love for Me. When I see My love in your heart return to My heart I become undone.

See also:

*Hosea 6:6, John 15:1-13,
1 Corinthians 13:1-3;13*

What Do You Treasure?

Matthew 6:21

"For where your treasure is, there your heart will be also."

What you treasure in this life tells Me where your heart is. Do you treasure My love for you? Do you treasure My Presence and our time together? Do you cherish what I give to you, the grace I bestow upon you by My Spirit? Do you treasure what My Son did for you; His body broken for you? How precious AM I to you? Of what worth AM I to you?

Am I worth more to you than your career, than your marriage, than your ministry? What is My value to you? My heart longs to be treasured; it longs to be rejoiced over by you, for I treasure you and long to be treasured by you in return. My child, if only you could see how much I treasure you, how valuable you are in My sight. If only you could see how precious you are to Me.

So many of My children treasure so many other things apart from Me. They treasure the world but the world does not treasure them. The world does not long to nurture you and hold you close, and delight in you. My children treasure others and the thoughts and opinion of man so highly, but no man or woman on earth will ever or could ever treasure you like I do. So why cherish these things more than Me, when what I offer you in Myself is far greater than what anything or any person can offer you? Why treasure what can never truly treasure you back as I treasure you?

You will sense as you are treasuring and delighting in Me, that I AM also treasuring and delighting in you. We are treasuring each other. How this delights Me, when you My beautiful child, delight in Me also. How this relishes my heart, when you My precious child, relish your heart in Me also. The deeper you treasure Me, the deeper My pleasure will be. Cherish Me as your greatest treasure, for I treasure you more than you could ever know.

If you treasure something or someone else greater than Me, I AM no longer in your heart, for your heart has left Mine to treasure that thing, that person. For where your treasure is, so your heart will be also. How much do you treasure Me? Am I in your heart right now?

See also:

Deuteronomy 7:6, Zephaniah 3:17, Ephesians 5:29-30

Captivated By You

Song of Solomon 4:9

*"You have ravished my heart,
My sister, my spouse;
You have ravished my heart
With one look of your eyes..."*

My eyes are always on you. I cannot take My eyes off of you. You have Me captivated. My focus is always on you. I AM continually waiting for you to turn your focus to Me.

I AM waiting for the moment when your eyes look to Me, to My Son Jesus. For when you are looking into the eyes of Jesus, you are looking into My heart.

So often My children are looking everywhere else but Me. They are looking at their circumstances, their bank account, their problems, their entertainment, but most of all they are looking at themselves. But that beautiful moment when My child looks away from the world and from themselves, and unto Me - how My heart rejoices! How heaven sings! For now the one My attention is always focussed on is staring back at Me!

Right now, I am lovingly gazing at you, and how I long for you to gaze upon Me! As you gaze upon

Me, you will begin to see as I see. A wave of My Presence and Glory will begin to fill your being as you behold Me through My Son Jesus.

You will see that the problem which has been consuming you, does not consume Me; the offense that you were holding onto, has no hold over Me. All that is within Me, is in My Son. In Him, is no problem, no bitterness, no fear; and you will see as you gaze upon Him, no problem or fear lies within you. All is well in Him, so all is well in you.

Do you know that I never grow tired of you? I watch you night and day in all that you do, for you have captivated My heart. Every thought, every feeling, every response of yours has My full attention.

But I am not watching you from a distance. I AM right by your side - right this moment. You do not realise the nearness of My Presence because your eyes are on yourself. Turn your gaze upon Me and you will begin to know the intensity and closeness of My gaze upon you.

See also:

Psalm 34:15; 119:37, Song of Solomon 2:9, Colossians 1:19

Wait for Me, Treasure Me

Psalm 37:7a

"Rest in the LORD, and wait patiently for Him"

The word 'relationship' has been so overused that it has lost its meaning. You can have a relationship with someone but they do not know your heart and you do not know theirs. I want more than a relationship with you. I gave My Son to die for you so that you can know Me intimately, not to be an acquaintance or just another relationship you have in your life. I gave My Son for you so that you could be made one with Me; so that you would give all of yourself to Me as Jesus gave all of Himself for you.

My child, I want you to feel My breath on your life, I want you to sense My arms surrounding you. I want you to know, to experience who I AM; to know My desire for you. I want to hide you away; just you and Me. Come to Me now and sink into My embrace. Come and begin to know My heart. It is for you.

But do not rush knowing Me. Do not push or force coming to know Me. This opposes Me. It is My delight to reveal Myself to you when you seek Me but intimacy with Me cannot be pushed or forced; it is progressive and it is beautiful; unfolding over a lifetime.

To seek Me is to wait on Me. Many of My children seek Me in a hurry – they fail to see that I never like to rush revealing Myself. I wait for the perfect moment for you to receive Me but few rest and wait for Me.

As you are waiting for Me, the purer and deeper your seeking and longing for Me becomes. I do not keep you waiting because I delight to see you wait, but because I know the precise moment when My Presence will touch you the greatest and fill you the most. Those who are hungry for Me will be filled.

While I long for you and your attention, I will only share with you glimpses of Myself and My heart that I know you can come to understand, for I know you deeply and know what you need.

If you treasure what I show you of Myself, and seek to know Me more, then I will show more of Myself to you as you surrender more of yourself to Me. You will find I do not keep you waiting so long because I can sense the hunger in you for Me is pure.

I love unfolding Myself to My children, I delight in it. I work together with the Son and the Spirit to share Myself with you. You cannot come to know Me in your own strength, it is only by the Holy Spirit who enjoins us together.

If I reveal My heart to you and you ignore or downplay what I have revealed to you by My Spirit, then I am reluctant to show you more until I can see you want to know Me more. But if you treasure and esteem what I reveal of Myself to you, even if it is the smallest of glimpses, then I will show you more and more and more until you can receive no more. For some, I will show them as much as they can bear.

It hurts Me too much to lay out My heart to someone who does not treasure it, who treats it as a cheap thing. This is why who I AM, My heart, is mostly hidden to the world and is only known by those who desire to know Me intimately, for this is what I rejoice in.

I do not rejoice in showing Myself to My child and being ignored. While My Spirit may keep revealing things to some who continually ignore Me, there is a point where I will withdraw until that one comes to Me and seeks Me out. Then, I know I can trust them with what I show of Myself to them.

For others, I test to see what is in their heart to see if they really want to know Me or whether they are seeking Me for their own gain. I AM a Holy God and I want closeness with you. I want your love but I AM not to be taken advantage of. I will bless those that delight in knowing Me but I know when someone comes to Me and does not want to know Me or love Me, they only want what I can give them. They love me with an agenda, a hidden motive, but motives of the heart are never hidden from Me even if they are hidden from you. I see your every motive before you see it yourself.

My love for you has no agenda. I do not love you for what you can give Me. I love you because you are My child. I want you to love Me simply because I AM your Father and I AM your God.

See also:

1 Chronicles 28:9, Isaiah 40:31, Lamentations 3:25, Luke 9:23-24, Hebrews 11:6, 1 John 3:16

Stillness

Psalm 46:10

"Be still, and know that I am God"

Do you know what I need to do to get some of you to be still? Only when the stirrings of your soul are quietened can you hear My voice and know Me. Some of you are stirring and striving to know Me and have intimacy; you are trying with all your heart but you must cease this stirring; leave it behind and then you will know Me.

Don't dwell on, "I want to know You, I want to know You." Just dwell on Me. There is a difference. When you are striving in yourself to know Me, the focus is still on you. To know Me, you must be still. When you shift your focus and behold Me and not what you want, then you receive the desire of your heart in knowing Me. Change the statements in your mind that say, " I, I , I, I want this, I want to do this, I want that", and shift your focus to Me- "You, Father, are wonderful. Father, You are faithful, You are full of loving kindness".

As you shift your focus from yourself and your desires, to Me, then by My Spirit you will begin to sense and experience Me. Your thoughts will soon be overtaken, and a stillness will surround your awareness; you are knowing Me. Know that whenever your focus is on Me by My Spirit, when you are dwelling on Me, I AM delighting in you. You are meeting with Me. We are joined together by My Spirit.

I AM known in stillness. Your heart, mind and soul will be stilled as you come to know Me. In this stillness, you will begin to forget about your strivings and ambitions; you will leave them behind and begin to sink into Me. As you sink into Me, the stillness will intensify and you will begin to sense My peace. When you meet with My peace, rest here in this moment and enjoy! Don't strive or question, just rest and enjoy what is found in Me! Soak here in My embrace, for here I will pour into you all that you need to be sustained and equipped by My Spirit.

I know what lies ahead for you every hour of the day. I know what is coming and I know what you need. What you need is to be still and know Me, for from this place of My embrace you will receive all that you need.

In stillness is total trust. How I delight in those that trust Me for I know this is true love for Me, for love always trusts. In stillness is My strength. When you are resting in Me, the bond between us is being woven over and over; it is strengthened. You and I are being woven together by My Spirit.

Jesus died for you so that no veil is between us. Come to Me now through Him, and let your soul find stillness in Me. I AM waiting.

See also:

Psalm 34:8, 2 Corinthians 3:13-16, Colossians 3:1-4

Living Water

John 4:14

"but whoever drinks of the water that I shall give him will never thirst."

When you gaze into My eyes and look into My heart, you will see the pools of Living Water that live deep within Me, and you will be able to drink of Me and My beloved Son Jesus.

In Me is life. Drink deeply. Draw out of Me all that you need. Draw out of Me all the wholeness you long for, all the love you have been searching for. It is all found in Me. Draw it out of Me. My supply is limitless. Do not look elsewhere for what you lack. Look to Me, your Father, your Provider, and I will provide for you from the glorious riches found only in My Son Jesus.

And what riches I have stored up for you My precious child! The whole human race can draw their entire sustenance from My riches, and still it is not a drop in the ocean to Me. My storehouse of spiritual riches is abundantly supplied. I AM a God of abundance and I delight in supplying you with all that you need. I delight in being your Provider. I delight to bring you what you need as you draw deeply from the Living Waters found within Me.

There is a pipeline that you can draw from to My supply. This pipeline is a mystery but My Spirit will make it known to you. My Spirit will show you how to draw into this pipeline and teach you how to live from the abundance of My supply, so that no matter what circumstances you face on earth, you are never in lack. You are connected to My constant abundance- the abundance of heaven.

All the riches of all the sultans and kings of this world from the beginning of time until the end of this age, do not compare to the riches found in My Son Jesus. But My riches are not earthly riches, they are spiritual treasure with no earthly price. You cannot buy them on earth; you cannot earn them – they are freely yours because of what My Son Jesus accomplished. Believe in what He did for you on the cross and drink deeply of these riches. Draw deeply from Me all that you need. Siphon it into your inner being by My Holy Spirit and be filled. Be made whole.

I want to fill you to overflowing. I want to fill you with the glorious riches, the lavish treasure of Who I AM and what is found in My Son Jesus. Do not look anywhere else, be still and drink. Draw in deeply all that I have for you.

This Living Water comes from My Throne Room; it comes from heaven and it is life. Let your thirst be quenched by the Living Water that is deep within Me. Drink deeply of heaven's abundance. Receive all of your sustenance and satisfaction from Me. When you drink deeply and are sustained by Me, you can then show others to Me and bring them My life. It is all from Me.

The more hungry and thirsty you are for the Living Water, My life that is found only in Me, the more you will siphon from Me, the quicker the outpouring will come and the quicker you will be filled. If you are hungry for things of this world, for things of this age, then you are drawing your life from the world. You are trying to be sustained from the world and the world cannot sustain you. The world cannot satisfy you. The world will only make you more hungry and thirsty for its fleeting pleasures, which are short lived.

You cannot draw your life and satisfaction from the world and from Me. You must choose which power you will draw from. Draw all your sustenance from Me alone and you will know true contentment and fulfilment. Draw from Me and live.

See also:

Psalm 36:8-9, Isaiah 55:1-3, Matthew 5:6,
John 4:10-14;10:10, Ephesians 3:19-20,
Revelation 22:17

You are My Delight

Psalm 139:13,14a

*"For You formed my inward parts;
You covered me in my mother's womb.
I will praise You, for I am fearfully and
wonderfully made..."*

Even now I AM looking into your eyes, staring at the precious creation that I formed before the foundation of the earth. I cannot help but think of how much I love you; how much I adore you.

Do you know that it was always My perfect plan that you would love Me and live with Me forever? Do you know that when I created you, long before you were born, I was excited and delighted over you? You were made for My pleasure, for My delight. I made every part of you out of love. I fashioned you with My own hands. You are Mine. I created all My children before the foundation of the earth in this way. I longed for the moment when you, My child, would be able to have the mental faculty, being of age, when you could choose yourself to respond to Me; to want to know Me as I know you. I have waited for this moment. I have longed for it; but for most I am still waiting.

It breaks My heart when those that have opportunity to know Me, reject Me. I send My Word to them so they may hear of My truth and come to know Me, but they reject Me. They reject My love.

I AM the God of unrequited love. Despite the vastness of My love, the vast majority is unrequited. It is not claimed; it is ignored, forgotten. My intense desire for My children so often never returns to Me.

How My heart delights when I find a child who delights to receive My love. Who cherishes it and treasures it, and longs for more. Truly My heart sings, and My pleasure and power rests upon this one who delights to know Me and My love.

I have a measure of My love, a portion set aside just for you. This portion of My love is more than you will ever need or know, but it is especially for you. It is marked by Me and it comes from Me. It comes from My heart and you experience it by My Spirit

I have been waiting since before you were born, since the foundation of the earth, to share with you My love which I set aside especially for you. No one else will experience this part of My love. It is a part of My heart just for you, waiting to be experienced, to be known. Do you want to experience every day the love I have set aside for you, that comes only from Me?

You cannot beg for it or strain to receive it. My love comes freely to you by My Spirit. You cannot try and make My love come to you- it is already yours, you simply do not believe.

My Presence will wash over you like a wave when you accept that My love is yours. If you do not believe My love for you, you will not receive it. Rest in the knowledge that I love you, believe it and you will experience My love. And as a result, you will experience My delight! For I delight to shower those who believe in Me with My love!

See also:

Isaiah 43:1,4; 64:8;
Jeremiah 1:4-5, Romans 5:5, 1 John 3:1

How I See Sin

Isaiah 59:2

"*But your iniquities have separated you from your God;
And your sins have hidden His face from you*"

Do you know how much I detest sin? How much it grieves Me? With the same intensity and strength of My love towards you, so is the intensity and strength of My indignation towards sin for it separates Me from the one I so deeply and passionately love - you. How can I be indifferent to something that pulls away from Me the one I love? To say that I AM indifferent to sin is to say that I AM indifferent to you and that is not possible.

And in My eyes, sin is all the same. It is all detestable. I do not want you anywhere near it. I do not want you playing or toying near anything that may lead you to sin and separate yourself from Me.

Do you know that My heart broke in the Garden of Eden? I had created My son Adam and daughter Eve in love. I had made the most exquisite beautiful paradise that no garden you now see on earth could compare to. We had fellowship together. I was so pleased. All was complete, but they chose to sin instead of fellowship with Me. I was rejected. My heart was broken.

The same choice is being made every day. My children are choosing sin over Me and My heart is continually breaking.

What grieves Me even more is when My children think that I am pleased with them when they sin. They are deceived. I cannot tolerate sin. I reject all of it. It is not part of My Kingdom. I will not allow it to enter. All sin is darkness to Me. It is black.

But you My child, have no reason to fear or be condemned. You have overcome sin when My Son Jesus died for you. My Spirit was sent to the earth to help you to see this. Sin now has no power over you. Sin has been conquered. Nothing separates you from Me when you believe what My Son has done and turn from your sin unto Him. His blood has brought you near. People do not see this, they think that they can come near to Me and keep sin in their life. I cannot allow it. I AM a holy God.

No matter how deeply I love you, you cannot come into My embrace, into My arms, and know My heart through any other way but the blood of My Son Jesus; for I AM a holy God. The blood of My Son purifies, makes you clean. It sets you apart and makes you holy, for I AM holy. Turn to His blood. Turn away from that vile sin and turn to Me. I AM waiting for you. Don't keep breaking My heart with that sin in your life.

You cannot love Me and still sin. True love for Me, when it is birthed by My Spirit, always produces the fruit of obedience. I will never put you in any temptation that is too great to bear, so you can always keep loving Me.

See also:

Genesis 6:6, John 14:15, 1 Corinthians 6:9-11; 10:13, Galatians 5:19-25, Ephesians 2:13, 1 John 1:5-10

The Kingdom of My Heart

Matthew 6:10

"Your kingdom come. Your will be done on earth as it is in heaven."

If only you would open your eyes and see the world that I have waiting for you in Me. The world that I want to share with you is in My heart. It is in My Son Jesus. You can know this world and live in this world, in Me, every day. I want you to; I long for you to. I never want you to leave. I want you to stay forever with Me in My heart, My Kingdom - the Kingdom that is within Me. This is your home. Your home is not in this world. Your home is with Me, in My heart, in My Son Jesus. Do you know what is in this world inside of Me? Do you want to see? Do you want to explore?

How much time do you give to Me, getting to know and experience Me and the world that is within Me and My Son Jesus? How much time do you spend getting to know and experience the world around you, with its vain amusements and circus of charades and actors? It is all a mirage. It is all an act. It is all falling away. My world is eternal. My Kingdom is everlasting. I want you to live with Me, in My Kingdom, every day of your life.

I want you to see yourself as I see you in this world as a prince, as a princess, reigning and ruling. My world's government has no end. It is not based on the fallen system and politics of today. I rule. I am in charge. My Son is the King. Everything in My Kingdom is done only according to My word and I will bring My word to pass. It does not come back void.

Only those who are living in My Kingdom, in My Rulership, will see My word come to pass and My promises being fulfilled by the power of My Spirit. My Kingdom will come to your earth as it is in heaven. But for My will to be done on earth, you must be living in My world, My Kingdom. My Kingdom is in My heart. Come to know My heart and live from there and you will see My will fulfilled here on earth.

The world that is in Me is not an amusement park. It is a Kingdom. Yes, in that Kingdom you will be delighted and your soul will feed off the abundance of My Presence, but you will also find refuge and obedience and food. It is not a place to come and go. It is your safe house, your fortress. It is for your very livelihood to live in My Kingdom. In My heart is everything you need. What is it you lack? You will find it in Me.

See also:

Psalm 145:13, Isaiah 9:6-7; 55:10-11, John 15:4, Romans 5:17, 1 Peter 2:9, 1 John 2:17, Revelation 1:5-6

My Kingdom in You

Luke 17:20-21

"*Now when He was asked by the Pharisees when the kingdom of God would come, He answered them and said, "The kingdom of God does not come with observation; nor will they say, 'See here!' or 'See there!' For indeed, the kingdom of God is within you."*

This world, this Kingdom within Me, is at hand. You do not need to strive to look for it. It is already within you, for when you are in My heart, you and I are one. All that is within Me, is within you. Everything that is in My Son Jesus, is in you now by My Spirit.

In you, are all the treasures of heaven, for in Me are all the treasures of heaven. All the riches of My Son Jesus- an everlasting hope that endures all things, a peace that goes beyond all understanding; a joy that triumphs over all adversity; spiritual riches that money can't buy. These riches are found within you through My Son Jesus. He became poor, humbling Himself on the cross to the point of death so that you could become rich My child! And what richness awaits you in My Kingdom My precious one!

People do not see this treasure of Mine within them because they do not believe it. They only see themselves. They do not see what I have placed in them by My Spirit. When you look within and only see yourself, then so you will only live from yourself and your own natural limitations. But when you look within and see Me and My Kingdom, the glory of My Son Jesus, and the power and might of My Holy Spirit, then you can live from My infinite provision.

The Kingdom of heaven is at hand. My Kingdom, My heart, is closer than you think. It is within you.

See also:

Matthew 10:7, John 17:20-24, Ephesians 1:3-9; 18-23, Philippians 2:5-9; 4:19

My Treasure in You

Luke 11:13

"*If you then, being evil, know how to give good gifts to your children, how much more will your heavenly Father give the Holy Spirit to those who ask Him!"*

Yes, I have placed in every one of My children, in every one in My Kingdom who accepts the work of My Son Jesus, an amazing treasure. Treasure you would never believe or imagine. When you surrender to My Spirit and trust in Me, this treasure begins to shine through you. The world begins to see its glistening. They begin to see My Son Jesus in you. They begin to see My Kingdom in you. For this treasure within you is a piece of My heart, it is a part of Me within you.

What is this treasure? It is My Holy Spirit, whom I gave to you as a gift. He is the greatest treasure the earth has ever received! It was My Holy Spirit that conceived Jesus your Saviour in Mary's womb, and that raised Him from the dead to grant you victory over sin and death. It is My Holy Spirit who draws you to Jesus and to My heart.

What a mighty treasure the gift of the Holy Spirit is! When I see My Spirit in you, I see My Son

Jesus. I see perfection. I see righteousness. Let My Spirit, the greatest treasure you will ever come to know, shine through you so that others may be drawn unto Me and My Kingdom. He is ever present to help you now!

See also:

*John 14:26, Ephesians 1:13-14,
1 Corinthians 2:9-12,3:16, 1 John 2:27*

My Way is the Greatest

Isaiah 55:9

*"For as the heavens are higher than the earth,
So are My ways higher than your ways,
And My thoughts than your thoughts."*

You must understand that I only ever have the best for you My child. I delight to see you blessed. I delight to give you what you long for. But you must understand that I know the end from the beginning. I can see dimensions and aspects far into your future that you do not know or perceive. You can never assume how I will perform My will but you can trust that it will be done when you remain in My Kingdom. Don't ask how. My will always leads to My best for you. It may not look like My best from the dulled perspective that you see when you are focusing on natural circumstances at single points in time; but you do not see as I see. From what I see, from My perspective, I know that I am taking you into My greatness.

I will order things and allow circumstances to take place never to crush you but to draw you closer to Me, so you have greater opportunity and capacity to know Me. Embrace these opportunities to know Me. For I am drawing out of you My best for you. I AM forging in you the likeness of My Son Jesus so you may also draw more people unto Me.

You must understand that nothing is ever a surprise to Me. Nothing. Nothing is ever a shock to Me. I know and perceive every reaction and response and thought of yours long before I created you. How I long for you to respond to Me so that you may bring Me delight.

My greatest delight is when you look to Me and love Me despite your circumstances. Only when you love Me despite what you experience around you, can the light of My treasure begin to shine from within you; so the world may begin to see Me in you. Then the world will see that He who is in you truly is greater than all else; and so they may begin to know Me and the greatness of My way.

See also:

Psalm 139; 1-4,16, Proverbs 16:3, Isaiah 46:9-10, Romans 8:28; 11:33, 1 John 4:4

Layers of My Love

Ephesians 3:18-19

"*may be able to comprehend with all the saints what is the width and length and depth and height— to know the love of Christ which passes knowledge; that you may be filled with all the fullness of God.*"

There are so many layers, so many facets of My love. You cannot count or measure them. They are infinite. Each layer of My love grows in greater intensity and depth. Greater height, greater length, greater width and greater depth - so the revelation of My love grows for you. Come and know My love in each layer that there is. The deeper and longer and wider and higher you see that My love is for you, the more you will come to trust Me. The more you will know that you are loved. My love is always centred on you My precious child.

My love has no end. It has no beginning. It always was. It always will be. It is eternal. It cannot be stopped, it will not relent. It will not give up. It will not fail.

My love is of heaven. When you encounter My love you encounter heaven, you encounter Me.

When you show other's My love, you are showing them heaven and you are showing them Me. Love is the language spoken in heaven. Love is the language I speak to you. My Spirit speaks only love.

Love takes different forms, it is not one dimensional, My entire nature is found in My love. But do not think for a moment that because I AM love that I do not bring punishment; that I do not chastise or rebuke. For all these come from My love. My nature is to maintain My Holiness and My Kingdom, and love brings you into My holiness and My Kingdom. Love also stops anything that goes against my Holiness and My Kingdom so that My holiness and My Kingdom are maintained.

This is why I chastise those I love, I want them to experience and know Me in greater measure, to know My power and the fullness of My Kingdom. When something is stopping you from moving forward in knowing Me and My Holiness and having My Kingdom displayed in you, I will intervene. When someone repeatedly refuses to know Me and goes against My Holiness and My Kingdom, I will intervene and I will Judge. This is My nature and this is still My love. What kind of Father allows rebels and terrorists to sleep in the same house as His children? I cannot allow rebels, those who purposely sin against Me and defile themselves, to sit with Me and dine with Me and My children, in My Kingdom for eternity to come.

But even for that rebel, I still love them. I still yearn for them. My heart still breaks for them. And so I will send My Spirit to convict them to turn to the blood of My Son Jesus, then they can sit with Me and dine with Me and My children, in My Kingdom for eternity to come.

See also:

Psalm 57:10; 63:3, 1 John 4:8, Revelation 3:19

Turn to Me

Ephesians 2:13

"But now in Christ Jesus you who once were far off have been brought near by the blood of Christ"

If you only knew how I hunger for you. How I desire you. My hunger for you does not wax and wane depending on what you do for Me. I do not love you more when you serve Me or less when you deny Me. My desire for you never changes; its intensity never weakens.

Do you think that I do not hunger still for those who have denied Me and chosen sin over Me? Do you think I have forgotten them? No, they may have forgotten Me but I will not forget them. They may have forsaken Me but I did not forsake them. I never stop desiring them and longing for them to return to Me before the consequences of their sin become final.

One of the greatest lies My adversary tells My children is that they do not have access to Me; that they are not worthy. That they do not deserve My love for them. It is true that you are not worthy, you do not deserve My love based on anything you have done or do because you cannot earn My love. But there is One who has made you worthy; One who has given you free access to My heart. My love is yours not based on what you do for Me but on what Jesus has done for you so that we can be together! I loved you so much that I made a way to bring you near to Me so we may never have to be separated; that Way is My Son Jesus. Through His death, you never need to be separated from Me again.

All sin is forgiven when you turn to My Son Jesus and keep turning to Him. When sin enters your life, turn away from it unto Jesus and you have free access to Me. Do not turn to sin, for by doing so you are turning away from Me and My love for you. Turn to Jesus, the WAY to My love and I, in My love, am freely yours.

You, who have continued to sin in secret, know that it is no secret to Me. Soon all will be brought into the light. I see what others do not see. I see your impatience within. I see your unforgiveness; your bitterness; your pride; your lust. While your sin separates you from Me here on earth, I do not want it to separate you from Me for all eternity in eternal torment. You must understand that the consequences for sin are eternal. At the Day of Judgment, My decision is final.

Turn to Me now from your sin before it is too late! Turn to the blood of My Son which washes you clean and brings you near! Turn now, for once your life is no more and you are in eternal darkness, there is no turning back. Fulfil My desire for you and turn to Me.

See also:

*Deuteronomy 31:6, John 14:6, Romans 8:1-4,
Hebrews 10:26-27; 13:5*

My Love is Stronger

Romans 8:38-39

"For I am persuaded that neither death nor life, nor angels nor principalities nor powers, nor things present nor things to come, nor height nor depth, nor any other created thing, shall be able to separate us from the love of God which is in Christ Jesus our Lord."

There is a mighty pull of the world that lures My children unto sin. There is a mighty pull of the flesh and the demonic that pulls My children unto wickedness and idolatry. There is a mighty pull of fear that lures My children to doubt and panic. But there is an even mightier pull, a greater drawing, a greater tide that is stronger and more powerful than any force known in heaven or on earth. It is the drawing in of My heart unto yours. It is the strength of My desire for you.

When you are surrendered to My Spirit you will perceive it. My heart calling unto yours. Drawing you away from sin and the world and unto Me, unto My heart. How strong My yearning is for you. How strong My desire is for you to come closer to Me.

I will never force you to come to My heart, but I will draw you- oh how I will draw you! I will draw you with words, with songs of deliverance, with the beauty of My creation, but most of all I will draw you with My love. My love is the most powerful force in all creation. It has overcome all sin, all darkness, all temptation, all devils, all evil, all fear, all sickness. My love will never fail you. My Son has won victory over all by His blood, and now nothing can come between us.

Do you perceive it? This mighty pull of My love is drawing your heart unto Mine right now. It is stronger than the sin you feel so entangled in. It is stronger than the lust that you think you cannot let go of. It is stronger than the fear which attempts to consume your mind. My love is infinitely stronger than all.

Let go of that darkness, it has no hold over you. What has hold over you is My love. What is holding you right now is My hand; My arms; My embrace. I will never let you go. If you surrender to My love; to My embrace, it will take over you. My love will truly be the centre of all if you allow it to be. Let Me pull you closer in by My love, which is found in My Son Jesus and what He did for you. Can you sense it now? Can you sense the mighty pull of My heart drawing you in now? Come to Me. The only thing stopping you is yourself.

See also:

Song of Solomon 1:4, Psalm 32:7, Isaiah 46:4, 1 Corinthians 13:8

My Word

John 21:25

"And there are also many other things that Jesus did, which if they were written one by one, I suppose that even the world itself could not contain the books that would be written. Amen."

My Word is life. It is My heart for you but it is not all there is to Me. There is so much more to Me than what is described in Scripture. All of who I AM and all of what I, My Son Jesus, and My Spirit have done, cannot be put into one book. All the libraries of the world would not have room to fill all the books that could be written of who I AM. I AM indescribable. I could fill all the libraries around the world with revelation describing My love and it still would only be a mere taste. The revelations available of who I AM are never ending.

Right now, the saints in heaven cry in adoration and praise of Me and My Son for all eternity, and are still growing in revelation of who I AM as they worship Me! Revelation of who I AM never ends because there is always more to be revealed of Me.

Here on earth, My Word is condensed, concentrated truth for you to live by. My Word is Me. When you are hungry for My Word, you are hungry for Me. If you are not hungry for My Word then there is iniquity in your heart that must be purged. Hunger for Me and hunger to know Me will always lead to a hunger for My Word.

See also:

Psalm 119:11; 15-16; 49-50, Matthew 4:4, John 8:31, Hebrews 4:12, Revelation 4:10-11

Looking Right Through You

1 Corinthians 6:17

"But he who is joined to the Lord is one spirit with Him."

When I look at you My love, My dove, I AM staring right through all the layers of your flesh and soul, and I AM looking right into the deepest part of who you are- your spirit. I, your Father, am spirit and I long to commune with your spirit, the deepest part of you. I cannot commune with your flesh, your body or your soul. I AM Spirit and I yearn to be one with your spirit.

You cannot connect with Me with your intellect or just with your feelings, I yearn for a deeper connection. Let my Spirit weave your spirit into Mine and make us one. By My Holy Spirit, your spirit and My Spirit are made one through the blood of My Son.

Your spirit always loves Me and yearns for Me as it is made in My image. The deepest part of you is always longing for Me. If you do not long for Me or desire Me, it is because you do not listen to your spirit. You listen to your soul or your flesh which oppose Me. Listen to the deepest part of you, your spirit, by the Holy Spirit, and you will see that you were born to be one with Me. This is how I created you. When we are apart it goes against My will for you. Your spirit was not designed to be apart from Me, for apart from Me your spirit begins to wither and weaken.

When you are in Me, living in Me, your spirit is satisfied and grows and produces beautiful fruit which I delight in. It is all done from the deepest part of you - your spirit; the part of you which always has my full attention and the part of you I long for, because this is the core of who you are.

You are not your body, you are spirit. I long for you to worship Me in spirit, for this is the only true worship. You cannot know Me other than by your spirit.

See also:

Isaiah 26:9a, Luke 1:80, John 4:24; 15:5, Romans 8:16

To Know Me is to Become Like Me

2 Corinthians 3:18

"But we all, with unveiled face, beholding as in a mirror the glory of the Lord, are being transformed into the same image from glory to glory, just as by the Spirit of the Lord."

Do you know what I delight in? When I see Myself in you. When I see My Son who is in Me- in you. Those that want to know Me must realise that when you are knowing Me by My Spirit, you are becoming more like Me, My Son Jesus, who is the fullness of who I AM.

Are you willing to leave your old ways behind so you may know Mine? Are you willing to leave your old thoughts behind so you can receive Mine? Are you willing to leave your old emotions behind so you can sense Mine? The more you leave behind, the more you can receive the newness of Who I AM and become like Me.

You were made in My image and it is My desire that you and I are one. The more the eyes of your heart are on Me, the more like Me you become. What you behold is what you become. If the eyes of your heart are on fear, then fear will become you. If your eyes are on the things of this world, then worldliness, material things and temporal pleasures will consume you. If your eyes are on what you don't want to become or don't want to be, then so you will be it.

Keep your eyes on Me and My nature, and My nature will be yours. My nature will be your nature. My thoughts will become your thoughts; My ways, your ways, for we will be of one Spirit. Always keep your eyes on Me.

See also:

Genesis 1:27, Proverbs 23:7a, Matthew 6:22, Romans 8:29, Colossians 2:9-10, 2 Peter 1:3-4

My Beauty

Psalm 27:4

"One thing I have desired of the LORD,
That will I seek:
That I may dwell in the house of the LORD
All the days of my life,
To behold the beauty of the LORD..."

Do you know the beauty that awaits you in heaven? The beauty of My Kingdom; the beauty of My holiness. I AM preparing a place for you now that is more beautiful than your mind could ever begin to imagine. But the beauty of heaven is not the same as the beauty you see on earth. It is not of this world. It is a supernatural beauty that transcends any beauty that you have ever known; so concentrated, so pure, - glorious perfection for you to delight in for all eternity. This is the beauty of heaven, the beauty of My Kingdom.

But right now, you can encounter My beauty. For right now, I AM surrounded by beauty. I AM surrounded by loveliness. It is who I AM. I created beauty in My image.

All the beauty that you see on earth is to draw you unto Me. The fullness of My beauty today can be found in My Son Jesus. He is beautiful beyond any comparison on earth or in heaven.

He is beauty personified. So pure. So holy. There is no fault in Him. He is perfection.

When you behold My Son Jesus and bask in the beauty of His holiness, then His beauty will surround you. You will see His beauty in simple things that you had overlooked. You will see that His beauty and glory surrounds you now. You will see beauty in every woman and every man regardless of age or physical appearance because they were made in My image. You will see them as I see them.

Beauty is more than just appearance, it is a state which is so pure and perfect that it draws the heart. It inspires awe. This is the beauty I created. A supernatural beauty that captivates, that draws unto truth. Supernatural beauty does not flaunt or parade itself, true beauty invites and welcomes, because it awakens the heart to search deeper into what it beholds. It nurtures the eye of the beholder, for whoever perceives true beauty with the eye of their heart, reflects what they see. The longer My children behold the beauty of My Son in His holiness, the more they will reflect the beauty found within Him. This is true beauty.

True beauty which is only found in Me and all that I AM in, is to draw you and invite you into My Presence. I want to captivate you. I want you to be one with Me in the beauty of My holiness. Will you stay beholding the purity of My beauty which is everlasting, and allow yourself to become captivated by My Presence? Or will you dart your eyes to the world and its superficial lusts, which charm the senses but destroy the soul?

I want to add beauty to your life. I want to adorn you with all the purity and splendour of My Son Jesus. I call you beautiful, for you are. For when you are in My Son Jesus, you cannot be anything else but beautiful.

Let Me adorn you with My beauty. Look to Me and be adorned with My Majesty, which is so lavish yet so pure and perfect, in the beautiful holiness of My Son Jesus.

See also:

Song of Solomon 1:15; 4:7; 5:10-16, Isaiah 61:10, Matthew 13:45, John 14:2-3, 1 Peter 3:3-4

Grounded In My Love

Ephesians 3:14,17

"For this reason I bow my knees to the Father of our Lord Jesus Christ….that Christ may dwell in your hearts through faith; that you, being rooted and grounded in love"

Satan will do all He can to destabilise My church. To shake My children. To get My children to take their eyes off the Rock on which they stand, and onto the shaking circumstances around them and others. My child, you must know that nothing can ever shake Me and when you put your trust in Me, nothing can ever shake you.

All the powers in hell cannot move a single hair on your head unless I allow it. All the powers in hell cannot make a petal of a flower fall unless I condone it. For My power is supreme. My power and My greatness are unshakable.

My children who do not believe in My greatness, will react to outward circumstances and Satan's attempts to destabilise the church, in extremes. The first extreme is when My church senses the destabilisation, but reacts out of fear, with over zealousness. They will attempt to control in the flesh and stabilise the church by manipulating people and circumstances around them through fear and condemnation. Fear will not draw people to My heart. These ones attempt to draw people away from outward circumstances and to go inwardly, but the inward pull is from the wrong source. These ones have a fear of Me that is not by My Spirit, but a lying spirit of religion.

The second extreme is seen when those in My church become so caught up in the outward cares of the world and being within the outer destabilisation itself, that they are not aware of the repercussions that are happening inwardly in their spirit. Those in this camp will become very complacent to My life, and will stop seeking Me, but rather increase their soulish and fleshly appetites. Religion will also prevail in their heart and many will not perceive the inward change. These ones will not fear Me, nor obey My Word.

Those in the centre, those in My true church, who will not be moved or shaken, those who are My unstoppable army, are those who are rooted and grounded firmly in My love. They will react to the destabilisation by simply drawing deeper and closer to the Rock, to Me, their Father, whom through Jesus Christ makes all things work together for good. These ones will fear Me by My Spirit for who I AM, and will fear being separated from Me because of their love for Me. They will obey Me because of their love for Me, not out of fear.

What is the point of building a church if it cannot weather a storm? The storm coming will actually be a catalyst to show the world that My true Church, those devoted to Me and obedient to Me, will not only weather the storm but be a shelter for others and a lighthouse that will shine brightly to show the true Way unto Me. Those rooted and grounded in My love will rise up and thrive in this destabilisation, for I will only fortify even more the very ground on which they stand and put their trust in. They will truly shine as their eyes are not taken off of Me, for My brightness never fades or weakens.

These ones I will send by My Spirit to help unveil the deception of the other extreme reactions in the church. Their witness will draw My church back to Me. My church doesn't need a lecture or head knowledge, it needs Me, it needs to know Me, to encounter Me personally- to know My love. Only My love will draw My church to My heart. Only My love will keep My people close to My heart and My ways.

Only My love will save you and keep you My child. Only My love.

See also:

Isaiah 60:1-5, Joel 2:1-2, 11,
Matthew 5:14-16; 7:24-25

Your Invitation to the Father's Heart

Your Invitation to the Father's Heart

God the Father loves you so passionately that He wants nothing more than to have you close to His heart, living with Him for all eternity. To remove the veil of sin which separates you from Him, He sent His only Son Jesus to die for your sins, and be raised from the dead, so that you could have an intimate relationship with Him, now and for all eternity (John 3:16).

It doesn't matter if you have been to church your whole life or if this is the first time you have heard of God; the only way to have closeness with the Almighty Father and experience His love now and for all eternity is through the life of His Son Jesus Christ.

Jesus is waiting for you now to surrender your life to Him by the power of the Holy Spirit, so that you may experience the fullness of relationship with the Holy Trinity.

If you want to accept the Father's invitation and receive the Person of Jesus Christ into your life, simply pray the following prayer with all your heart:

Dear Heavenly Father,

Thank You for sending Your Son Jesus to earth to die and rise again for me, so that I may know You.

I turn away from my sins and my old life and surrender my life completely to You now, Jesus. Come into my heart and cleanse me with Your precious blood. I receive Your forgiveness.

Jesus, You are now my Saviour and Lord. I belong to You- my heart is Yours forever. God Almighty, You are my Heavenly Father and I am Your child. I am now born again!

Fill me with Your Holy Spirit. I give You permission to have Your way in every area of my life. Help me to live every day to please You alone.

In Jesus name I pray, Amen.

If you prayed this prayer with all your heart- congratulations! You have no idea the wonderful world that awaits you in the heart of the Father, through Jesus Christ!

The word says that we must confess our faith in Jesus (Romans 10:9). If you prayed this prayer, I encourage you to tell someone (preferably someone who also has a relationship with Jesus) about this eternal decision. Find a Spirit-filled local church and start reading God's Word, the Bible, to learn more about who God is.

The fact that you have accepted Jesus does not mean that your life will suddenly be without problems. The difference is that now, regardless of what circumstances you face, you can be confident that your Heavenly Father is with you, and surrounds you with His love and protection. His Holy Spirit, your Helper, is ever present to help and lead you to victoriously overcome anything that opposes you, through the wondrous work of Jesus Christ.

Above all else, remember to always cherish your Heavenly Father and to love Him with all of your heart, for He greatly, so greatly, treasures and adores you!

www.ingramcontent.com/pod-product-compliance
Lightning Source LLC
Chambersburg PA
CBHW072104290426
44110CB00014B/1814